HISTORY in a HURRY

Tudors

written and drawn by
JOHN FARMAN

MACMILLAN
CHILDREN'S BOOKS

First published 1997 by Macmillan Children's Books
a division of Macmillan Publishers Limited
25 Eccleston Place, London SW1W 9NF
and Basingstoke

Associated companies throughout the world

ISBN 0 330 35254 7

Text and illustrations copyright © John Farman 1997

The right of John Farman to be identified as the
author of this work has been asserted by him in accordance with the
Copyright, Designs and Patents Act 1988.

All rights reserved. No reproduction, copy or transmission
of this publication may be made without written permission.
No paragraph of this publication may be reproduced, copied or
transmitted except with written permission or in accordance with
the provisions of the Copyright Act 1956 (as amended). Any
person who does any unauthorized act in relation to
this publication may be liable to criminal prosecution
and civil claims for damages.

3 5 7 9 8 6 4

A CIP catalogue record for this book is available from
the British Library.

Printed and bound in Great Britain
by Mackays of Chatham plc, Kent

CONTENTS

Off we go! What happened When		4
1	The Historical Bit	6
2	Those Wives	10
3	England v France v Spain	13
4	After Henry	15
5	Good Queen Whatever	20
6	Travel – Gadding About in Tudor Times	26
7	Inns and Alehouses	30
8	Fun and Frolics down the Local – Tudor Theatre	33
9	Who was Who and Where did they Live?	35
10	Who did What to Whom	41
11	Education – Teaching the Tiny Tudors	49
12	Tudors Tuck In	54
13	At the Doctor's	58
Time's Up		64

OFF WE GO! WHAT HAPPENED WHEN

1485 Henry VII (Henry VIII's dad) becomes first Tudor when he beat Richard III (who lost his horse) at the battle of Bosworth.

1492 Columbus risks slipping off the edge of the world and discovers the West Indies (accidentally).

1509 Henry VIII becomes King of England and starts hiring and firing (and beheading) his wives.

1547 Little Edward, Henry's only boychild, becomes the VIIth when only twelve days old.

1553 16-year-old Lady Jane Grey becomes queen – it was a nine day wonder.

1553 Mary Tudor becomes queen, executes Jane Grey and her hubby, then burns all the Protestants she can get her hands on.

1558 Royal bastard Elizabeth becomes queen.

1568 The Spanish send an Armada because they didn't like Elizabeth I executing Mary Queen of Scots who they wanted as queen!

1568 (also) Sir Francis Drake, fed up with this world, sets off to find us a nice new one which, when found, they call . . . The New World.

1603 Elizabeth dies, mad as a snake, but having united her people.

End of the Tudor dynasty.

PS. If you notice some irritating scribbles by someone calling themselves 'Ed' in these pages, I'm sorry, but it's Susie, my fussy editor*. The printer left them in by mistake and we didn't have time to change 'em before printing the book.

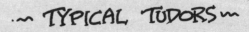

*Just doing my job! Ed

Chapter 1
THE HISTORICAL BIT

The Tudor age started in 1485 after a huge civil war between the Lancastrians and the Yorkists, both based up North, which seemed to be about the colour of roses and the egos of two great dynasties: the Yorks and the Lancastrians. Civil wars were a great way of settling arguments and keeping the population at bay. This one ended in a sort of a draw when Henry VII, a Lancastrian, got it together and married Edward IV's girl Elizabeth, a Yorky (amazing how marriages are almost as good as civil wars at settling arguments!).

To Have or to Have Not
There then followed a golden age, making most others in England's colourful history pale into baleful boringness, with a cast-list that a Hollywood director would drool over: Henry VIII, Will Shakespeare, Elizabeth I, Tom Wolsey, Laurence Olivier* to mention – er – five.

Golden, because it was practically the first time an exploding birthrate was matched by a healthy surge in the economy. If you have one without the other you're usually in for big trouble (see India, China or Wandsworth). But to be strictly accurate** it was only really golden for the landowners (the Haves), as your average peasants (the Have-Nots) had to watch their living standards plummet (essential supermarket consumables rocketed by 488% in the century following Henry

---
* Wasn't he just a Shakespearean actor? Ed
** A rare treat, Mr Farman. Ed

VIII's accession). Funny thing, progress, it always seems to be the poor that pay for it. Ah well, c'est la vie.

Henry VII

The Tudors officially started with Henry VII from the House of Lancaster: he was the one who beat the cruel and unpopular Yorkist Richard III in 1485 and promptly married Elizabeth of York to make England one big happy family again (having neatly snitched all the Yorkist lands). He still had loads of enemies, however, but gradually managed to show them who was boss by outlawing their private armies, not letting them have any castles, holding on to all the best weapons and taxing them to the hilt.

SORRY MATE, YOU'LL HAVE TO TAKE IT DOWN AGAIN.

Henry reigned peacefully for thirty years and made England very rich which was very nice. Better still, he forced one of his daughters to marry the geriatric King of France (on condition that she could have a husband of her choice when he keeled over), his other daughter to marry the King of Scotland and, best of all, his eldest boy Arthur, to marry the King of Spain's daughter Catherine (of Aragon). This, in theory, made everyone dead matey. Arthur, unfortunately, hardly lasted long enough for a couple of decent Spanish holidays at his father-in-law's place. His dad, mean as they come, refused to give the dowry money back on his son's death, and rather cheekily promised her to his next son, Henry.

This to-ing and fro-ing caused all sorts of rumpuses (rumpii?), but we're in a hurry, however, and the Tudors to come are much more fun. We'll press on.

Happy Birthday, Henry VIII

When Henry VII died, Henry Jnr, the King's old youngest son, but now the King's new oldest son because the old oldest son had popped his clogs, got the key of the palace door, together with a big golden hat, a kingdom, the surname 'Eighth' and a slap-up party throughout the land, all on his eighteenth birthday (beats my Boots gift token and free half at the Dog and Dungheap).

Being clever, handsome, virile and rather anxious to get on

with things, he quickly steamed in and married his ex-older-brother's now ex-wife,* Catherine of Aragon (the King of Spain's daughter), and invaded France (more of that later).

Useless Fact No. 12
Henry VIII was the first monarch to eat turkey.

* Oh please, not again. Ed

Chapter 2
THOSE WIVES

Girl or Boy?
In those days the main duty of being a wife was to have a son, because a) they were thought to be best (any comments, girls?) and b) a man-child helped secure the family line in the foreseeable future. Anyway, Catherine ended up with five kids – mostly girls and all of 'em dead except for one called Mary. This displeased Henry no end, not because they were dead but because they were girls (presumably even *dead* boys were better than dead girls). Poor Cath was, by this time, looking more than a little babied out (not to mention the stork), so Henry made up some cock-and-bull story about the marriage not being valid in the first place (strangely forgetting to mention he fancied a maid called Anne Boleyn in the second place). This really annoyed the Pope, who'd pulled a few strings to allow the blinking marriage in the place *before* the first place*.

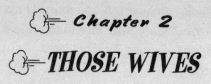

Divorce for Gain
He promptly told our 'Enery that he was excommunicated (can't be a Catholic any more). Henry said 'Get lost!' (in as many words) and promptly made himself the boss of the

---

* What? Are you going mad? Ed

Church (removing the heads of, or burning, anyone who disapproved). This turned out to be rather a fab move financially, as it now meant he'd inherited (a nice word for stolen) the church's vast fortunes – almost a quarter of all the wealth in England. He later got rid of all the monasteries for good measure as he was pretty sure the monks wouldn't be too thrilled about him being their new boss.

Five More to Go

Henry quite got into the idea of hiring and firing women, and by the time he died, aged 56, he'd got through six wives – two of whom had to suffer a little head-removal because he simply couldn't think of another way to get rid of them. Anne Boleyn, for instance, his second, just couldn't get the hang of having male children either (unless you count the one that died) so Henry, who for some time had thought her a bit of a witch, promoted her to a proper one. He also tortured his wife's personal lute player into confessing that he'd slept with her three times and then had both the lute player and Anne beheaded (and also a couple of other supposed lovers just for good measure). Anne's legacy, her daughter Elizabeth, was however, to be one of the greatest queens of England ever.

Useless Fact No. 15
Anne Boleyn became commonly known by the commonly folk as the 'Goggle-Eyed' or 'Great' whore. Her daughter, Elizabeth, was rather charmingly referred to as the 'Little Whore'. (and we think we're disrespectful to our Royal Family). This was because the great English public thought that Catherine of Aragon should still be queen, and therefore those two legitimate children of Anne Boleyn's were regarded as not.

If you want to remember their various names and their various fates, remember this rhyme:

Divorced, Beheaded, Died,
Divorced, Beheaded, Survived

Catherine of Aragon (*divorced*),
Anne Boleyn (*beheaded*),
Jane Seymour (*died*),

Anne of Cleves (*divorced*),
Catherine Howard (*beheaded*),
Catherine Parr (*survived*).

Chapter 3

ENGLAND
v
FRANCE
v
SPAIN

To cut a long story (as well as all the people that got in his way) short, Henry VIII's reign was reasonably peaceful for the English at home. 'Abroad' was far more concerned with the ongoing tussle between the Spanish and the French over who would control the Continent (Europe, to you). England had always had a problem with the French (nothing's changed there) so Henry sided at first with the Spanish (run by his first father-in-law), and had several not bad, if somewhat small (and strangely expensive) wars against the French, their mates the Scots, Emperor Maximilian of Germany and practically anyone foreign who could raise an army.

All Change

Henry then decided that he quite liked the French after all, and together they had a war against Spain in 1528, until the whistle blew and everyone changed ends and rejoined their original sides. We, therefore, teamed up with Spain again to fight the French (again). Business as usual, I suppose.

The War Game

Wars, in those days, were not so much about politics or territory as hard, take-home cash. It was big business. If you won, you inevitably brought back a lot of loot with you, but if you lost, you didn't – and wars were horribly expensive things to lose. Henry VIII started well but gradually squandered the huge wealth that he had inherited, by not getting enough clear results in many of the wars that he fought. And who had to pay? You've got it. His poor downtrodden subjects through more and more punishing taxes.

When Henry died, aged 56, in 1547, he left an England totally broke but oddly united and even a bit cocky. He also left his only son Edward (out of third wife, Jane Seymour*) engaged to his sister's granddaughter, the weeny queenie Mary of the Scots (queen from one week old). As we will see, things soon went from bad-ish to worse-ish.

---

*You make her sound like a racehorse! Ed

Chapter 4

AFTER HENRY

Bad to Worse

Poor little Edward VI (born 1537 and brought up Protestant because his dad had given up being a Catholic) became king at nine, an age when he'd far rather have been playing with his train set* than trying to keep the Protestants and Catholics apart. As for ruling a country that had totally lost the plot economically – forget it. The natives were looking decidedly ugly.

His first Protector and advisor, the Duke of Somerset, was actually fairly dreadful but was soon replaced (due to his execution) by the Duke of Northumberland who was even worse. For a start, Northumberland, being a bit of a baddie, wasn't much of a God man (even though he made it law that everyone else was), and proved it by systematically robbing all the churches of what was left of their finery. He then got the now decidedly dodgy (healthwise) Edward to bequeath his crown to a young girl called Lady Jane Grey who was – surprise – married to Northumberland's son. Edward didn't

---

*Er, I'd hate to state the obvious but trains – of any size – weren't invented until the nineteenth century. Ed

find this too difficult as he was known to loathe his two sisters – the rightful heirs.

Lady Jane (who was, by all accounts, a real babe) only hung on to the crown for nine days before she and her hubby (who she hated) were given the guest suite in the Bloody Tower because the English had had quite enough of rotten Protestants. 'We want a Catholic next,' they cried, and got their way. Mary Tudor, daughter of Henry's first missus, Catherine of Aragon, was crowned in 1553.

Spanish Twist

So what did Mary do? She went and married some blasted Spaniard named Phil. Not any old Spaniard, mind you. This Philip was soon to be king. So England became Catholic again. But the fickle English, you'll be surprised to learn, didn't find life any better under that lot. Mary, you see, had begun by executing 274 high-ranking Protestants, starting with Lady Jane and her husband (who must have wished by then he'd never married her) and then, for good measure, Northumberland, Jane's father-in-law*.

Useless Fact No. 21
Lady Jane Grey still haunts the tower of London (happily reunited with head). I wonder what happened to the ghosts of the other 273?

Mary then declared war on France once again (a right regular royal pastime) and this time England lost hands down. She died in 1552 and everyone had a huge pi— er – drink-up, to commemorate the event.

---

*I've a headache coming on. Ed

Useless Fact No. 22
Mary Tudor became so paranoid about assassination that she started wearing armour – even in bed.

Lizzie's Turn
Remember Elizabeth, headless Anne Boleyn's girl? In 1558 her name came up next to sit in the grandest seat of all, even though she and her (now dead) half-sister Mary had always been referred to as the 'royal bastards' (don't ask me why*). But England was in a worse state than ever economically, and there was that young Mary Queen of Scots to worry about.

M Q of S was the granddaughter of Henry VIII's sister Margaret (are you keeping up with all this?) and loads of people, especially the Catholics, thought *she* should be queen. Elizabeth naturally thought she shouldn't, and had her head cut off (on the principle that you can't wear a crown if you ain't got a head to put it on). Mary, by the way, had rushed down from Scotland, where things had been going very wrong, to seek the friendship and protection of Elizabeth (see Bad Errors of Judgement in Tudor Times).

Useless Fact No. 23
Mary's head was put on display in a window at Fotheringhay Castle the moment it was chopped off. Her lips apparently moved grotesquely for a quarter of an hour (any suggestions as to what she might have been saying will be duly considered).

*Why? Ed

Elizabeth, as you've probably worked out, was a Protestant, and she had a fine old time getting the Catholics back for what they had done to her lot, by severely punishing their priests for silly misdemeanours like altering altars and wearing hats.

Philip Gets Tough

Philip of Spain (dead Mary Tudor's old hubby) had a lot of gripes with our Elizabeth, the least of which was the murder of his wife's cousin's daughter Mary Queen of Scots*. He was also fed up with our fleet buzzing around the West Indies which he rather thought his territory, and Elizabeth's threatened support of the French against the Spanish. I reckon, however, that it was the fact that our Virgin Queen had turned her nose up at his cheeky proposal of marriage that really hacked him off.

> *Useless Fact No. 27*
> Messages in bottles were a rather haphazard method of communication in Elizabethan times. When Elizabeth heard that a boatman at Dover had opened a message bottle sent specifically for her, she appointed an Official Uncorker of Bottles. Any unauthorized bottle-opener was to be promptly executed.

*Do we really need all this? Ed

Proper War

Philip had finally had enough and in 1558 sent an Armada (Spanish for 'loads of warships') to get us. But with the help of Sir Francis Drake (who set fire to quite a lot of their galleons in Cadiz harbour), a damned great storm and unlucky loss of anchors when they reached England, the Armada was seen off pretty pronto – 80 ships and 10,000 men down (as in under the waves).

The war with Spain, however, cost galleon-fulls of money and dragged on right to the end of Elizabeth I's reign: the end of the Tudor dynasty. But we're not there yet! So pay attention. There's more about Elizabeth in the chapter on – um – Elizabeth.

Useless Fact No. 28
It is thought that the modern salute originated when the officer in charge, following the wondrous defeat of the Spanish Armada, ordered his sailors to shield their eyes with their right hands from 'the dazzling loveliness of Her Majesty' (Queen Elizabeth). What a creep!

Chapter 5

GOOD QUEEN WHATEVER

Elizabeth I is often referred as Good Queen Bess because a) she was reckoned to be good and b) Bess is short for Elizabeth. Of course, they could have called her Good Queen Beth, Good Queen Liz, Lizzie or even Good Queen Lilllibut, as all these are acceptable shorteni—*

Anyway, whatever they called her, I'm going to give her a chapter all to herself because she's probably the most famous woman in British history (apart from Boadicea, Margaret Thatcher or Barbara Windsor). She was legendary for three reasons, her political genius (she could get round anyone), her extremely long life (only two Tudor Royals lived beyond fifty), and most of all, the fact that she managed to stay a virgin throughout all of it (or so she said).

Childhood had been a touch tricky for young Lizzie. It's one thing hearing whispers that your dad had your mum's head chopped off, but quite another knowing that yours could go too – especially being second in line to a sister with a nickname like Bloody Mary.

On top of that, one of little King Edward's 'advisors', Lord Thomas Seymour, often tried it on (use your imagination) with his stepdaughter Elizabeth when she was only ten. On one occasion Seymour even set about Elizabeth's clothing with a pair of scissors – presumably so he could 'see more' (geddit?). When his own wife Catherine Parr (the one that survived

---

*Please get on with it. Ed

Henry VIII) died, he even tried to marry Elizabeth but she would have none of it. Just as well really, for he was soon to be executed by his brother, Lord Somerset 'verie daungerously' (you can say that again), 'yrksomelye' (execution *is* somewhat irksome) 'and horrybly' (any execution's a bit horrible) – for treason. Talk about Happy Families! What a waste of wedding cake *that* would have been.

When Edward died, Elizabeth's sister Mary (Bloody Mary to you) was made queen and Lizzie became first reserve. She got her chance aged 25 in 1558, when Sis died of cancer. The trouble was that the Catholics, especially abroad, still thought that Lizzie was the child of an unlawful onion* and a Protestant to boot. If that wasn't bad enough, everyone was dead nervous about her avowed intention to stay a virgin for the rest of her life, which meant that she would never have a straightforward heir (or anything else come to that). It also upset the Duc d'Alençon, Prince Erik of Sweden, Archduke Charles of Austria, the Duc d'Anjou, ex-brother-in-law King Philip of Spain and half Europe's aristocracy, who all proposed to her at some time or other.

*Shouldn't that be 'union'? Ed

Useless Fact No. 29
I wouldn't mind betting that the term 'Frogs' for the French comes from Elizabeth's nickname for the small, slimy and extremely ugly Duc d'Anjou. Lizzie was so into the way people looked that she made sure no ugly people were ever given a job in her household (I'm the same with my servants*), so the Duc was on a sticky wicket to start with.

Elizabeth wasn't daft, however, and was well aware that they weren't after her brain or body, but her country and cash. The execution of Mary Queen of Scots, daughter of her cousin James V of Scotland, actually helped her position with her subjects. Although some people thought it a mean thing to do to someone you're supposed to be looking after, it helped friends and enemies alike to realize that, like her dad Henry VIII, she was a chip off the old block (chopping block that is).

What Did She Look Like?
From all the descriptions I've read, she must have looked a bit like Vanessa Redgrave – tallish, dignified, not pretty but pretty striking, 'like a goddess' to her people. Her best features (depending on your taste) were her flame-red hair, pure white skin, trim (if a bit skinny) figure and beautiful, long fingers.

Useless Fact No. 33
Elizabeth used to dye her horse's mane and tail bright red to match her hair.

*You wish! Ed

Her worst feature was a long, slightly hooked, snooty nose. In those days, fair or red hair, a high forehead and a pure, dead pale skin was regarded as the ultimate in beauty and she had the lot. She was big on clothes as well. Lizzie was renowned for her collection of over 3000 opulent dresses (long way to go yet, Diana), the magnificence of which defied imitation, and for her hair, which was most times to be seen whipped up in a lavish concoction of precious gems and huge pearls held together by a gold net.

> **Useless Fact No. 34**
> Lizzie loved to dance, and there are some ridiculous paintings of her leaping high into the air (in full ballroom kit) while dancing the Italian Cabriole (I thought that was a car).

In later life, however, she must have looked well weird, having no eyebrows, practically no teeth and a terrible skin caused by constant use of white lead as make-up. She must have smelt pretty awful as well, as she seldom had a bath, and used copious scent instead. It is rumoured that she went bald due to smallpox and that from then on wore a bright red wig, one of the first ever known. She was obsessed by her looks, so much so that official portrait painters were issued with authorized face patterns in case they made her look too old. It became the fashion for all her sycophantic courtiers to wear flattering miniatures of her, set in pendants or brooches. Get your Fergie brooches here, folks!

> ### *Useless Fact No. 36*
> Tudor women were so nervous about getting a suntan that they would wear a mask held in place by a button between the teeth. Don't ask how they spoke.

What Was She Really Like?

Some of her critics described her as 'proud', 'disdainful' and 'bossy' but, to my way of thinking, if you can't be like that when you're the Queen (and with a nose like that) when can you? Others thought her very clever, very composed and, best of all, very witty. Mind you, I should think you'd have needed your wits about you with the executioner continually breathing down your neck.

Her worst habit was that she drove everyone totally bonkers, changing her mind about absolutely everything every five minutes. She could also be extremely irritable if she didn't get exactly what she wanted and was constantly complaining about being ill. Her temper was such that when one of her courtiers 'broke wind' on bowing low, he had to leave the court for seven years. When he returned, she laughed saying, 'My Lord, I had forgot the Fart.' I bet *he* hadn't.

> ### *Useless Fact No. 40*
> The queen often showed uncharacteristic devotion to her subjects. There was a common complaint called 'The King's Evil', a nasty disease that sufferers thought could only be cured by the monarch's touch. Elizabeth would press their sores and ulcers with her long white fingers as she passed through the towns and villages. (Can you see our lot doing that? I can't.)

Lizzie's Last Days

As Good Queen Bess got older, she became more and more eccentric and grumpy. She would constantly hobble round her rooms, bald, toothless and wigless, plunging her rusty old sword into priceless wall-hangings and furnishings, convinced assassins were poised to jump out on her. She would veer between tearfulness and rage, and even spat at a young courtier who got up her nose.

Chapter 6

TRAVEL...
GADDING ABOUT IN
TUDOR TIMES

If you think our roads are far from perfect now, you should have tried travelling in the 16th century. In fact, even calling them roads is going a bit far*, as most were just muddy tracks; gooey in winter and horribly rutted in summer. A few stretches of the old dead-straight Roman roads still existed (why aren't all roads straight?) but, as the Romans had packed up and gone home over a thousand years earlier, they were becoming a little the worse for wear. In 1555 an 'Act for Mending the Highways' ordered parishes to maintain the roads running through them, but nobody seemed that bothered: let's face it, most country folk didn't go anywhere much, so why spend time or money on visitors or travellers?

Where am I?
If having no proper roads wasn't bad enough, there were hardly any signposts, which meant that not only did you find it difficult to get anywhere, but when you did get

*Like calling you a historian. Ed

somewhere, you didn't know where you were or where you'd come from (does that make sense?). As you can imagine, your average troubled traveller was easy pickings for muggers, highway robbers, Happy Eater Restaurants.* Not to mention the roving gangs, sometimes eighty strong, of rowdy vagabonds (Liverpool supporters?) who shifted aimlessly around the country.

The reason for all these desperate, wandering yobs was the gradual switch from wheat growing to the less labour-intensive sheep rearing which had put thousands out of work. Also, the Dissolution of the Monasteries (Henry VIII's work) meant that impoverished peasants, orphans or wounded ex-soldiers could no longer get handy handouts from the monks when desperate. Worse than that, there was no dole in those days.

Useless Fact No. 42

Jack Horner was steward to the last Abbot of Glastonbury. When the monasteries were dissolved in the 1530s, the Abbot sent Little Jack to suck up to old crosspatch Henry VIII. Jack took with him a ginormous Christmas Pie, containing the deeds of twelve manors (a bit like the coins we get in our Chrissy puds) as a present for the King.

Naughty Jack couldn't wait to get to London but before he got there he 'stuck in his thumb' and removed . . . the deeds to the Manor of Mells in Somerset for himself.

His rellies claim that it's all a nasty lie and that the nursery rhyme existed way before Tudor times. (I prefer this story, however, and it's my book.)

*Please! Ed

Darkness Falls

Night driving was far more dangerous as horses in those days had no headlights and the cats had no eyes. So the intrepid, tried and tested Tudor traveller usually aimed to do his journeys in small bursts, only attempting distances that could be covered by a fresh horse* during daylight hours. This led to a vast network of inns, stretching all over England's green and most-times pleasant land, which were built throughout the second half of the sixteenth century. Food, drink and a good night's sleep were available to all (who had the cash).

How It All Worked

Have you ever wondered exactly how they organized horses for long journeys, how they remembered when they got to their destination whose horses were whose, where they'd picked them up, and exactly where they'd left them? Easy, it went like this!

*As opposed to frozen? Ed

Say you wanted to go visit your girlfriend who lived in York over 200 miles from your home in Shepherd's Bush, and you were fairly sure your own past-its-sell-by-date personal horse would be well-knackered before you'd even got to the outskirts of town. What you had to do was plod along to the nearest inn and rent a 'post-horse' for around 2p a mile to take you to the next inn, 10 or 15 miles up the road. Usually you'd get a guide thrown in, who'd escort you and anyone else who wanted to go that way. The same guide would then bring all the horses back after they'd had a nice rest, and this time they'd be ridden by people who wanted to go the other way.

Neat, eh? It meant that you'd do your whole journey in little jumps. Having said that, I think I'd get a girlfriend closer to home if I had to go through all that malarkey.

Chapter 7

INNS AND ALEHOUSES

Just *Inn* Time

Inns must have been real welcome if you were a Tudor traveller. Huge and half-timbered with bustling stables, ostlers (who looked after the 'orses) and buxom serving wenches rushing hither and thither across the straw-strewn courtyards. Visitors usually arrived covered in muck from the filthy road (or the filthy horses) in need of rest, a hot bath and a hot meal. Many of these inns could accommodate over 200 people so, unless you had the same luck as Joseph and Mary*, you'd be taken to a room where a maid would tend to your every wish (yes, even that too, sometimes**).

The larger inns competed to outdo each other in service, food and entertainment, a bit like our fabulous motorway stopovers (I don't think).

But they weren't all respectable. Some of the inns, as you can imagine, were pretty disgusting and tip-off haunts for highwaymen looking for easy victims. But not as disgusting as most of the notorious alehouses.

Mine's a Flagon

Actually alehouses sounded a bit of a riot; dens of iniquity, usually run by one family. Despite their reputation, the law said that the following were forbidden:

---

*That's another story! Ed
**Careful! Ed

- 👑 The playing of unlawful games and gambling.
- 👑 The harbouring of rogues, vagabonds and common criminals.
- 👑 The lodging of women about to be delivered of bastards.
- 👑 Engaging in the business of brothel-keeping or housing prostitutes.
- 👑 The serving of food or drink on the Sabbath.

. . . in fact, all the things they usually DID!

Useless Fact No. 48
A West Country Justice of the Peace wrote that two louts had come up in front of him, who'd stayed in an alehouse for three weeks. During that time they apparently got through twenty fat sheep (they stole one a night) and ruined a poor peasant's ploughing by eating his ox. Talk about biting the ox that feeds you.

What's Yours?

Drinking alcohol was a big Tudor problem and the consumption of huge amounts on a regular basis was extremely common (you should visit my local!). The main drinks in the ale-houses were sack, a strong white wine flavoured with spices, and beer, of which there were many varieties and strengths. These ales had brill, enigmatic names like 'huffcap', 'mad-dog', 'father-whoreson', 'dragon's milk', and the rather ominous 'lift-leg.'

Useless Fact No. 49
The Elizabethans drank over 30,000 barrels of foreign wine each year (but not each!).

Chapter 8

FUN AND FROLICS DOWN THE LOCAL - TUDOR THEATRE

Theatre Inns
Actors and the theatre have always had a bit of a dodgy reputation, but none so bad as in Tudor times. It had all started with Henry VIII's terrible bust-up with the Church of Rome and the breaking up of the Church and Guilds. They'd been the only people to put on plays (mostly religious, mostly moralistic and mostly boring). With the growing popularity of inns as meeting places, bands of travelling players used them to put on their performances. The location was pretty good, as most had courtyards surrounded by balconies that were perfect for viewing. If these travelling companies didn't have licences (which magistrates were loath to give) they would be regarded as no better than rogues and villains and were often hounded out of town.

Large performances became a magnet for prostitutes, bear-baiters, cock-fighters, pick-pockets, child abusers, seducers of innocent maidens and so on. And some of the plays themselves were rude to the point of lewd. The relationship between the actors and their audience often became a running battle with fruit and rotten vegetables and even fireworks flying both ways throughout the performances. Sounds quite a laugh, doesn't it? Certainly beats all that Andrew Lloyd Webber junk.

Useless fact No. 53
Queen Elizabeth loved bear-baiting and had her own personal bear-pit and her own personal bears. She had a kennel full of vicious mastiffs which were set on the bears three at a time. She also, rather oddly, loved watching her pet monkeys fighting with horses. All that and she always claimed to be an animal lover. With friends like her, they certainly didn't need enemies.

Don't you think that in a chapter on Entertainment in Elizabethan times that we should just maybe mention the most famous playwright ever? Ed.
No. JF.

Chapter 9

WHO WAS WHO AND WHERE DID THEY LIVE?

The most important thing to remember, if you were going to survive in Tudor times, was to know your place. From the very bottom of society up, good manners (or should I say crawling to your superiors) meant the difference between working and not working, and in some cases, starving or not starving (and therefore living or not living).

By the time Elizabeth came along, just over halfway through the Tudor period, there were four million people and twelve million sheep in England (about three each – by my reckoning*). Most of those four million (90%) were farmers and their peasant labourers who worked themselves to a frazzle to support the other 10% – the lawyers, scholars, clergy, doctors, merchants and the small bunch of glittering aristocracy.

To the Manor Born
Most villages and small towns would have a manor house in which would live the local 'lord of the manor'. These were enormous, half-timbered and very posh (like their owners**), usually surrounding a lofty 'great hall' which, in earlier days, would have been used to house all the servants. Later, they

---
*Brilliant at maths as well, I see. Ed
**Half-timbered owners? Ed

were hung with dusty old pictures of all the master's early rellies and the rusty suits of armour that various old soldiers had gone to battle in (and most-times died in).

By mid-Tudor times servants had become a bit uppity and were demanding less draughty quarters, so the great halls were only used for feasts, dances (see Cold Balls) and other special occasions. Although these manor houses weren't as over-the-top as the huge palaces like Hampton Court, built for royalty and ministers, they were in a different league to the yeomans' farmhouses, being smothered in carvings of lions, dragons, coats of arms, gargoyles and all that sort of flashy stuff. The Lords of the Manor(s?) usually had to have fairly posh visitors' quarters (with separate kitchens), as by late Tudor times there seemed to be a whole bunch of sponging dignitaries touring the land with their attendant servants, blatantly looking for places to stay for nothing.

Queen on Tour
Queen Elizabeth, for instance, spent most summers touring her land, pitching up at whoever's grand house she favoured and staying for as long as she liked (great way of saving money). The good news was that it was highly rated to have the Queen stay at your gaff (prepare the spare room, I say). The bad was that when she travelled, she brought with her 400 wagons and 2,400 pack-horses carrying all the royal valuables, tableware, clothes and linen. Also, there were her servants and grooms, seamstresses, laundrywomen, clerks, cashiers, cooks, bakers, confectioners, butlers: all in all, over a thousand people. Gosh, that's almost as bad as my mother-in-law coming to stay.

Here's an average shopping list for a five-day Queen Visit: 60 sheep, 34 lambs, 26 pigs, 18 calves, 8 oxen, 10 kids (of the goatular variety), countless game birds, 350 chickens, over 200 pigeons, 12 dozen ducklings and herons, 10 dozen geese, 16 dozen quails, copious capons, curlews, pullets, partridges, mallards and shovelers and a couple of swans for good measure. Blimey, that's more than my mother-in-law gets through. And that's not counting the booze – but we won't go into that*!

As the procession proceeded through the countryside the common folk cheered and prostrated themselves at Elizabeth's feet. They simply adored her. Let's face it, if you're going to have a queen that costs a packet, you might as well have a really flash one (Windsors take note).

*Makes a change. Ed

Yeomen and Yeowomen

Between the Lords of the Manor and the peasants were the yeomanry, who generally owned and farmed their own land. All good yeoman needed a good yeoman's wife who was expected to do absolutely everything in the house. If a relatively respectable and moneyed man could have advertised in the local 'lonely hearts' column, the ad would read something like this.

Respectable middle-aged yeoman requires

Wife

Applicants must be able to:

cookmealsprepareandcurefoodforfutureuseorganisestoresbrewandstorealescourandpolishutensilsspinandweaveclothmakeclothesforthefamilyembroiderandsewthelinendistilperfumeandpreparecosmeticspreparefamilymedicationsgrowandknowhowtouseoverthirtyorsoherbshaveaknowledgeofmidwiferycareforandteachthechildrentendthekitchengardenandbeehiveslookafterthedomesticanimalsmakethecreamandcheesepaytheservantskeepthehouseholdaccountspolishandcleanthehousedothewashing AND ... be available for all those other wifely duties (if you know what I mean)*.

How's about that for a job spec, girls?

The largest proportion of people today are the middle classes. In Tudor times, there was really no such thing. The gap between the royalty/nobility/ministers/merchants/professional or landowning classes and the poor was enormous.

*We all know what you mean. Ed

Poorer Places

At the beginning of the Tudor period the accommodation of the poor was not, as you might imagine, exactly five star. Whole families would often live in tiny mud- and straw-built hovels with leaky thatched roofs and no chimneys. They would sleep in the dark, smoky squalor on pallets of straw, with logs for pillows and covers made of 'dagswain' (a rough blanket made from sheep droppings*).

The Great Rebuilding

By the time Lizzie came to the throne in 1559, things were looking up. The Black Death, which had done rather well for population control, was becoming a distant memory and the numbers were beginning to rise again (London's trebled in the 16th century). It became increasingly obvious that all these people probably (and somewhat inconsiderately) required feeding. Since England and Wales had 37,886,215 fertile acres (worked out by my sad mate, Keith, on his new personal organizer) it seemed rather silly not to use the surplus poor to work the surplus land to feed the surplus rest. This brilliant theory soon produced far more food than they needed, and when the government sold it off it gave them the spare cash for what came to be known as 'The Great Rebuilding'.

The Great Rebuilding (again)

Some of the hovels were simply given a facelift, but lots were simply knocked down and – yes – rebuilt. Most new cottages had a chimney running down the centre of the house. This would serve two fires for two separate rooms: the bedroom and the everything-else room – which would be located either

*Shouldn't that be clippings? Ed

side of a dividing wall – neat, eh! The slightly better houses would have a staircase running up beside this chimney, leading to two further rooms which were normally used for storage. All the other little areas, larders, bake houses, cheese-making rooms, jacuzzis, etc, would be stuck on to the side of the main house. Is this getting boring*? I think I'll stop here.

Useless Fact No. 55
Before proper lavs, the habit of keeping chamber-pots in cupboards and alcoves was referred to as 'p*ssing in chimneys'. The first flushing toilets in England were at the house of Sir John Harrington (the inventor). Harrington had been, rather appropriately, banished from Elizabeth's court for his lavatorial humour. As you might imagine, he had more than the usual amount of visitors, one of whom was the curious Elizabeth, who tried it out. She forgave him instantly – and ordered one for home.

*Just silly. Ed

Chapter 10

WHO DID WHAT TO WHOM

> **THIS CHAPTER IS NOT FOR THE SQUEAMISH.**
> **YOU HAVE BEEN WARNED!**

Everyone goes on about all the crime and violence these days, but compared with Tudor times we might just as well be living in a suburb of Toytown. They robbed and murdered each other as a matter of course, and there was no police force to control them. You might think that life would be quite a laugh without the police, but in practice, it meant that anyone could be pulled off the streets by chaps called 'watchmen' or 'beadles' and punished purely on someone else's say-so (come to think of it, things aren't that different *with* the police).

A Law for the Poor

By 1570 there were over 10,000 homeless and doshless, wandering about the country desperate to stay alive and not too concerned with how they went about it. A law had been passed in 1547 saying that all vagrants should be soundly whipped and sent back from whence they came (how about trying that, Mr Blair?): a neat way of dealing with another town's problems.

To deal with all this England and Wales used their 700 Justices of the Peace, whose job it was to make sure that people went to church (even if *they* didn't themselves), settle domestic arguments and try the accuseds in court.

Who Got What?

In the countryside petty theft, begging, dodgy shopkeeping or being caught in bed with someone else's wife (or sheep*) was dealt with by either birching or being chained in stocks to be pelted with rotten eggs and vegetables by those jolly, rosy-faced village folk. More serious crimes, however, were dealt with . . . er . . . more seriously.

If you wrote or published bad things about Royalty the usual punishment was to have your right hand cut off and the bleeding stump seared with a red hot iron (newspaper editors take note).

Useless Fact No. 57
One of the crimes guaranteed to get your neck stretched was called clipping – not illicit hairdressing or hedge-trimming – but the paring off of tiny fragments of silver and gold from coins to be melted down to make new ones – all the rage in Tudor times.

*What is it with you and sheep, Mr Farman? *Ed*

Which Witch?

Throughout the 16th century there was a craze for hunting down and murdering old ladies. Practically any old crone that lived alone with a cat (preferably black), broomstick (preferably twiggy) and a long, pointy nose (preferably warty), would be accused of witchcraft. And it wasn't just a British sport. Throughout Europe over 300,000 old dears were burned, hung or drowned because they were thought to be in collusion with the devil. If they wouldn't admit it, they were tortured till they did – and then executed into the bargain. I'm not sure what happened to the cats (or the brooms).

Useless Fact No. 58

Catch this. One of the methods of checking if the old dear was a witch or not was to fling her in the village pond. If she floated, she was guilty (and was then burned when dry), but if she sank, she was innocent (albeit dead).

Strangers in the Night

But all this paled into insignificance next to the carnage caused by religious or political differences. If you held a high position, or were simply a gentleman, you couldn't sleep that easy in your bed. Tudor times were rife with plot and counter-plot. One minute you'd be on the winning side, happily executing the opposition willy-nilly, and the next it would be all change and there'd be a knock on *your* door in the middle of the night.

This didn't usually affect the common man or his common wife. They thought it all a bit of a laugh. To them, having your head removed was simply one of the downsides of being born rich. But when ordinary guys like themselves did get caught up in the political intrigues, it all got a bit iffy. They were always being required to take sides, you see. At one time during Mary's reign, the rotting bodies of ordinary men who had misguidedly supported Sir Thomas Wyatt's rebellion against having a Spanish king (Mary's hubby), or who were simply following the wrong religion, would hang in scores like Christmas tree decorations outside the gates of major towns.

But London, then as now, being the entertainment centre of England, was treated to an even nastier spectacle...

Anyone for Stake?
As there was no footie, and if your average Londoner wasn't doing anything better on a chilly Saturday afternoon (and wasn't a staunch Protestant), he could do far worse than get himself down to Smithfield for a warm-up. Mary Tudor

(henceforth known as Bloody Mary – henceforth known as vodka and tomato juice) had made the discovery that those dry old Protestants burned rather well and to prove it she barbecued three hundred (sixty of whom were women) at Smithfield. First up were all the bishops (as you mitre guessed)*, and when they were well roasted, a whole crowd of clergymen followed. The last course was nuns (much sweeter), and then, practically anyone they thought might produce a good flame.

Useless Fact No. 60
If the executions were becoming a little routine, the Catholic executioners had a great way of livening things up. They sometimes tied bags of gunpowder to the legs of the doomed which made the proceedings (and the victims) go with a quite a bang.

But there was worse to come. Sometimes, simply executing your enemy wasn't enough, especially if you wanted to squeeze some information out of them...

How to Get Your Prisoner to Talk: Tudor Style

- First put them in a cold damp 'Dungeon Amongst The Rats' (a room at least twenty feet deep with no windows).
- If that doesn't do the trick, try the 'Little Ease' (a cell so small that your guest can't stand up, sit or lie down with any degree of comfort). Hopeless for those impromptu cocktail parties.

*Terrible joke. Ed

Useless Fact No. 66
The French, at the time, had an even worse dungeon called an 'Oubliette' (from the French for 'forget'). The poor prisoner was simply thrown into a deep well-like hole in the ground, a cover was put over it and then he was forgotten about.

👑 Still not talking? Try the 'pilliwinks' (to crush the fingers), the 'brakes' (to shatter the teeth) or the dear old 'thumbscrew' (to screw the thumb).

👑 Oh dear, oh dear. Still no talkie. How's about trying 'The Scavenger's Daughter': a neat bit of equipment designed to compress the victim's body with iron bars until all his ribs crack.

👑 My word, aren't some people obstinate? It's obviously time for the rack. This was a charming little machine that stretched the victim's arms and legs, inch by inch, until he, now somewhat taller, either spilt the beans (if he had any to spill), or saw his own limbs wrenched from their sockets. If that didn't make his eyes water nothing would.

Personally, I would have made a bog-awful hero when it came to torture. I'd tell anyone anything at the *threat* of a little light tickling.

Useless Fact No. 72
Queen Elizabeth was not averse to a bit of torture, and when Robert Holt, a priest, was 'racked' and then hung, the crowd noticed that he was mysteriously without fingernails (ouch times ten). It had all been on her recommendation (or should I say rackommendation?).

Family Fun

All that torture stuff seems like something you might see on *Blue Peter*, compared to what they did when disposing of political prisoners or conspirators. These executions took place in public and were very popular with all the family. I'll be brief, and I bet you'll thank me for it.

First the subject in question would be lightly *hung* (enough to throttle him, but not enough to kill him). Then he'd be *drawn* – that is, his innards would be pulled out from his tummy and his private parts severed from his body, much to the delight of all concerned (except, perchance, the victim).

Useless Fact No. 73
When Anthony Babington (accused of plotting to murder Elizabeth) was having his entrails drawn out in front of him, he was heard to mutter, 'Parce mihi, Domine Jesu.' Which my friend Cat, who did Latin at school, thinks means 'Pass me the dominoes, Jesus'.*

*She'd have to be a friend of yours. Ed

Four Places at Once

Anyway, after being 'drawn' the poor miscreant would be feeling none too well, so it was time for the old *quartering*, which involved cutting the 'patient' into four equal parts, which usually killed him. Each bit was then hung on a scaffold in the four corners of the city, just to remind the likes of you and me what would happen to us if we inadvertently found ourselves supporting the wrong side.

Chapter 11

EDUCATION – TEACHING THE TINY TUDORS

Uniform

Kids were regarded simply as adults of restricted growth, and were expected to behave as such (boring or what?). They were even dressed, almost from babyhood, in miniature versions of what their parents wore and must have looked – well – silly.

For instance, an aristocrat's son would be expected to put on something like – wait for it – a satin doublet with threads of silver and gold, velvet pantaloons, silk stockings, a soppy ruff round the throat, silver buckled garters, dinky little leather pumps, a velvet cap with a large feather sticking out of it and a silver studded belt with a little sword. Imagine turning up at school wearing that lot, lads. Poncy or what?

The offspring of your average poverty-stricken (or is that strucken?) peasant simply wore the same style of designer rags as their parents. It was the same with those in between the very rich and the very poor, whether a baker, a farmer, a blacksmith, an inn kee—*

No Point
There seemed very little point educating the peasants' children – so they didn't. Most of the population, therefore, couldn't read or write, which was not so bad as there was nothing to read and no one to write to (they only knew their neighbours). Posh kids would go to what were supposed to be free Grammar Schools (by the year 1600 there were 350 in England), which were all that was left of the education system after Henry VIII closed down the monasteries. I say 'supposed to be free' because when they became popular, the teachers would do cash deals with the dads and turn the whole thing into quite a nice little racket.

Late Start
Kids started school aged around seven, but because grammar schools would only take boys who could *already* read and write, before they went they had to attend what were known as 'Petty Schools' (from the French *petit* for small) or 'Dame Schools' (because the teachers were usually old women).

And the girls?
Girls, if they were lucky (and rich) enough to go at all, had to leave school much earlier, in order to learn how to be good wives and mothers (quite right too). Forget university.

*I think we get the picture, thank you. Ed

Early to Rise Makes a Boy Wise
The average day at the grammar school would go like this.

The day would start horribly early. After a quick brekkie the pupil would walk to school, lantern in hand, arriving between 6.00 and 6.30 a.m. (bad start, eh?). Lessons were usually held in an unlit, unheated hall and students would be overseen by ushers, who carried stiff canes or whips. (And you complain about your school?)

Each boy would have a 'hornbook' – a small wooden board like a table-tennis bat, which could also be used for games (or hitting each other with). On this would be a piece of paper with the alphabet, the Lord's Prayer and a brief guide to pronunciation. This sheet was protected by a thin piece of see-through horn (hence 'hornbook'). All writing was done with a quill which had to be regularly sharpened, spat on and dipped into thick black ink which would most-times spill, going everywhere, particularly the user's hands. As books were few and far between, a pupil would be required to memorize those that *were* around – word for word.

Useless Fact No. 74
Henry VIII banned all books on grammar, apart from the two he liked.
(That's kings for you.)

Lunch was at one o'clock, and although the food was boring, they'd probably get beer to drink (not bad, eh, lads?). After dozing through the afternoon lessons, the weary pupils' day would finally end at around five o'clock.

Home at Last

After supper, a quick read of the bible and a quick peek at Coronation Street*, parents and children alike would probably go to the bedchamber.

No late nights in those days.

Off to University

Very few poor kids ever got to university, but the ones that did generally had to act as porters ('sizars') to pay for their studies. These student porters did practically everything for the rich ones: cooking, cleaning, serving at mealtimes, getting them up in the mornings, brushing their hair (can you believe?) and some even wrote their blasted essays for them. (At least some things have got better!)

> ### *Useless Fact No. 77*
> These sizars were also called 'plebeians' (after the working-class Romans) which is where the derogatory term 'pleb' comes from, while the loaded ones were known as 'pensioners' (which I suppose refers to the fact that they didn't work for their income).

The tutors at university were also on to a darn good number. They'd take the new boys' jingly purses at the beginning of term in order to control their spending money (and their own fee).

The pensioners would have rooms to themselves but the poor sizars would have up to five in a room with only one bed – dodgy or what!** This was due to a clever rule that didn't allow them to board outside the college.

*It might be old, but not that old! Ed
**Thank you, Mr Farman. We won't pursue that, if you don't mind. Ed

The richer lads, as always, did
exactly what they liked
and spent all their
spare time at
common alehouses
or brothels with common
wenches, when they weren't
gambling at the local cock-
fights or bear-baiting rings.
Despite this they usually
managed to scrape through their
degrees (at a price).

Chapter 12

TUDORS TUCK IN

These days we can get frogs' legs from France, fish from Finland and oranges from – um – Israel* all at our local supermarket and at any time of the year. It was very different in Tudor times, as they could only eat what they could grow, and in winter, what they'd been able to store. Drying, smoking and preserving food is an art that has been largely lost because of the fridge and freezer.

This meant that the range of their food was very limited. Crikey, they probably couldn't have filled even half an aisle of one of our megamarkets. Kids had to drink beer with their meals as tea didn't arrive until 1650 or thereabouts and Coke wasn't invented till 1886. Chips were rather scarce, as the first potato didn't turn up until 1586 and coffee bars were deserted as nobody had even heard of coffee until 1652.

On the other hand, rather like the Chinese, they ate animals (and bits of them) that we wouldn't ever consider. Larks' tongues, cows' udders, baby eels, calves' feet, herons, blackbirds, swans – in fact, if it walked, flew or swam, you could pretty well bet they'd swallow it.

---

* Couldn't think of anything beginning with an I – eh? Ed
No, I couldn't think of anywhere beginning with an O. JF

Useless Fact No. 79

The Tudors thought it was a real hoot to bake a pie with nothing in it, and then fill the thing with live creatures – birds, frogs or even snakes who'd fly, hop or slither out as soon as the crust was broken. I don't know about you, but that'd make me chuck up, let alone eat. That, by the way, is how the nursery rhyme 'Sing a Song of Sixpence' came about.

Poor Food

Poor people ate poor but healthy food. Gritty bread made out of rye if they were quite poor, and out of ground acorns if very poor*. This they ate with vegetable broth, cheese, porridge and occasionally meat. Farm animals got a bit jittery around autumn: the peasant farmers couldn't afford to feed them through the cold, grassless winter months, so ate them instead.

Less Poor Food

Just to give you some idea of how well the non-poor lived, here's a typical menu for a modest family gathering. The assembled company would sit down for three to four hours at five in the afternoon and be brought:

The Starter

A salad of fresh lettuce dressed with vinegar and a little salt
(to counteract the inevitable heartburn from
what they were about to receive).

The Meat Course

A venison pasty served with sugared mustard
PLUS a shoulder of larded veal
PLUS a leg of mutton stuffed with garlic, all served with
cabbage and bread to soak up the gravy.

*Not as poor as your range of vocabulary. Ed

Now that would probably have done me,
but those greedy Tudors went on to:

The Fish Course
Locally caught salmon or trout
PLUS pickerels (baby pike)
PLUS salted herring.

Feeling a little queasy. Pause for music from
the village fiddler then off again:

The Game Course
A capon (small castrated chicken*) boiled with leeks
PLUS turkey-cock in pieces
PLUS a larded partridge.

. . . and to finish up:

Afters
A ginormous jelly surrounded by
candied violets and gilliflowers and
crushed flower petals soaked in rosewater.

All this was followed by a huge glass of
Alka Seltzer, before someone rang the
local take-away for a late snack.

Rich Food
Many things that were out of the reach of the poor *were* available, but only to the rich – who served them to show off

---

*Is it strictly necessary to mention that? Ed

to their smart mates. Oranges and lemons from the Mediterranean, turkeys from Turkey,* chocolate from Mexico, raspberries from Europe, wine from Italy and, most valuable of all, sugar from Asia. The sweet course of a posh Tudor meal was called a 'banquet' and often the most terribly tasteful of Tudors would have a 'banqueting house' in the back garden serving Turkish Delight (is *that* from Turkey?), sweets, little cakes and jellies which they adored.

*Everyone knows that turkeys came from South America (apart from you apparently). Ed

Chapter 13

AT THE DOCTOR'S

We all moan about the NHS today, but when you think that the average life expectancy in Tudor times was under 40 (for men) as opposed to well over 70 these days, it can't be all that bad. Doctors were known as physicians, and were few and far between. However, most minor surgery, from everyday tooth removal right through to amputation, was done at the barber's. (I can't see *Wayne's Hair Affair* in my local high street getting into that sort of thing.) Eventually a Guild of Barber Surgeons was set up, which meant that ordinary high street barbers were only allowed to cut hair.

Drugs as we know them (medical as opposed to recreational*) were very primitive. Most of the ones used today were developed in the last century, so the Tudors had to make do with a mixture of old wives' tales, the sort of herbal 'cures' you can still buy in health food stores and plain, honest, no-nonsense witchcraft.

Royal Health: HENRY VIII
From being a strong and athletic young man, Henry really let himself go and by his late forties was a shadow of his former self. Here are a few of the things that were wrong with him:

- He was thought by many to have suffered all his later life from syphilis, which could well have been caught from his ex-brother's wife Catherine, who was rumoured to have

---

*Don't you mean 'illegal'? Ed

indulged in some naughty behaviour with naughty Spanish priests.

👑 He became so horribly obese that throughout all his palaces, machines and ropes had to be installed to help him manage the stairs. Within five years the girth of his armour grew seventeen inches.

👑 He had fallen off his horse so many times that he had inflammation of the bone marrow, recurring headaches and even suspected brain damage (and a much relieved horse).

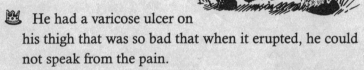

👑 He had a varicose ulcer on his thigh that was so bad that when it erupted, he could not speak from the pain.

👑 He suffered severe scurvy from not eating his greens.

👑 He was what we would call these days a manic depressive. (Who wouldn't be with all those problems?)

Useless Fact No. 81
When he died, Henry's body was so gross that it was difficult to get him into the coffin. The funeral service was interrupted by waves of disgusting smells that filled the chapel at Windsor.

Royal Health: EDWARD VI
Poor little Edward, Elizabeth's brother, when lying in bed suffering from a constant cough, swollen stomach, a festering

tumour on the lung, covered in ulcers and bed sores and being sick every five minutes, was prescribed the following:

Mix together sprigs of spearmint and red fennel, add liverwort and a turnip. Sprinkle in a few dates and raisins, followed by an ounce of nutmeg. Chuck in two heads of celery (sounds like soup so far) and – wait for it – the hind quarters of a nine-day-old piglet. Distil a liquid from this mixture and force nine teaspoonfuls down the helpless patient four times a day.

Unfortunately this odd little concoction had the opposite effect and in the end the poor little king's arms and legs became grotesquely swollen, his skin went dark (Michael Jackson's suffers the opposite), his fingers and toes began to rot, his hair and nails fell out and he became too weak to even cough. Apart from that he was fine! He died in 1553 whispering a prayer which probably went something like:

'Dear God, please keep those b***** doctors off me.'

Royal Health: ELIZABETH I

- 👑 She was extremely highly strung and often fainted from stress and breathlessness (from highly strung corsets?).
- 👑 Continual stomach pains, headaches and aching limbs.
- 👑 Frequent diarrhoea (not too good when you don't bathe much).
- 👑 Ulcerated legs.
- 👑 Gout in her right thumb.
- 👑 Swelling of the cheeks (facial) and constant toothache.

Useless Fact No. 83
Elizabeth was so obstinate about tooth removal that the Bishop of London allowed surgeons to extract one of his just to show how easy it was (that's devotion for you).

Bleeding Awful

Blood was seen as one of the keys to good health. Not the quality, but the amount (in those days blood was simply blood). Queen Elizabeth, who practically invented the word hypochondria, was constantly asking her quacks to tap blood from various parts of her body and was convinced it made her feel better. Failing that they'd use leeches, which would suck the blood out of whatever part of the body they were placed on (what a way to earn a living*). Oddly enough, centuries later, modern doctors are using the little critters again as they apparently have an ability to stop the bleeding as soon as they've had their fill.

*You can talk!

The Pox On It

Smallpox was the really nasty one in Tudor times. Usually it killed you, but if you were lucky you might survive – but you'd be left with a skin like the surface of the moon. Queen Elizabeth contracted the pox when relatively young and by the time the doctor got to her she was very poorly indeed. He used an old Arabian remedy which involved wrapping his patient from head to foot in a red cloth and putting her on a red mattress in front of a roaring fire. He then put a bottle to her lips (contents unknown) and told her to drink as much as she could.

Quite quickly red spots appeared on her hands (classic smallpox symptoms) and the queen was understandably well-miffed. The doctor nervously (for fear of head removal) told her she should feel lucky as they usually started on the face. He suggested pricking the spots with a golden needle, but they cleared up so fast that it wasn't necessary. Elizabeth's nurse, Lady Mary Sydney, wasn't so lucky. She caught the pox from her mistress and was left with a face like a pizza to prove it.

Nine Ways to Look Like a Tudor Babe

As we've said, the ideal Tudor girl would have fair or red hair, pale skin and a high smooth forehead. However the process that she had to go through to achieve this effect before going out, was often long and arduous.

1. First take a bath in asses' milk.
2. After bathing, apply liberal coatings of beeswax or ground hog's jawbone to the face. White lead mixed with vinegar, borax and sulphur gives the same effect, but beware as it has a habit of mummifying the face.

3. Apply lip colouring using red ochre, madder, red crystalline mercuric sulphide or cochineal (ground-up beetles).

4. Remove any skin imperfections like spots or freckles (regarded as extremely ugly) by applying a mixture of birch-tree sap, ground brimstone, turpentine and mercury (ouch!). Be careful as continued use not only removes the problem but half the face as well.

5. Apply a glaze of egg white to achieve the effect of polished marble. This one and number 4 were particularly good for hiding smallpox scars.

6. Pluck out any trace of eyebrows and paint thin blue lines on bosoms (often almost totally exposed) to represent veins (weird or what, girls?).

7. Drip belladonna (deadly nightshade) in eyes to enlarge pupils, then paint black kohl round eyes.

8. Scrub teeth vigorously with nitric acid, ground pumice-stone, brick-dust or coral.

9. Smother body in scents made from aloes, nutmeg (fine, if you want to smell like a rice pudding), marjoram, musk, rose-water, ambergris (fine, if you want to smell like a whale's intestine) or civet (fine, if you want to smell like a small furry animal's bottom*).

Blimey, so much for the natural look. With women looking and smelling like that I'm not surprised the Tudor dynasty didn't last.

*You're disgusting. Ed

TIME'S UP

I reckon (now I've finished the book) that living in Tudor times must have been pretty fab (providing you were rich and always on the right side of any wars). Sorry that it's a bit short, but seeing as you've only paid a couple of quid, and it took me ages* to write, I think you got a pretty darn good deal. Anyway, I hope you now know a little bit more about the Tudors than you did before (cos I'm not giving you your money back) and that you might even depart forthwith to find out more on the subject.

If, however, you've had enough of the Tudors (or *my* Tudors), why not rush down to your local bookshop and get another book in the series. If I haven't covered the subject that you're really interested in, be patient! I'm writing the blinking things as quick as I can.

*Who are you kidding? Ed